CW00348066

1 MONTH OF
FREE
READING

at

www.ForgottenBooks.com

By purchasing this book you are eligible for one month membership to ForgottenBooks.com, giving you unlimited access to our entire collection of over 1,000,000 titles via our web site and mobile apps.

To claim your free month visit:

www.forgottenbooks.com/free961880

* Offer is valid for 45 days from date of purchase. Terms and conditions apply.

ISBN 978-0-260-64755-9
PIBN 10961880

This book is a reproduction of an important historical work. Forgotten Books uses
state-of-the-art technology to digitally reconstruct the work, preserving the original format
whilst repairing imperfections present in the aged copy. In rare cases, an imperfection in
the original, such as a blemish or missing page, may be replicated in our edition. We do,
however, repair the vast majority of imperfections successfully; any imperfections that
remain are intentionally left to preserve the state of such historical works.

Forgotten Books is a registered trademark of FB &c Ltd.
Copyright © 2018 FB &c Ltd.
FB &c Ltd, Dalton House, 60 Windsor Avenue, London, SW19 2RR.
Company number 08720141. Registered in England and Wales.

For support please visit www.forgottenbooks.com

PREFACE.

So far as it concerns Canada, the battle against the Liquor Traffic was never waged more successfully than to-day. In the present struggle FACTS are the chief offensive weapons. Facts are said to be "God's arguments." In this case they have been unfailing in their effectiveness.

The Board of Home Missions and Social Service of the Presbyterian Church has prepared a somewhat comprehensive historical review of movements in various parts of the Dominion, governing the sale of intoxicating liquors. Competent students have carefully studied Provincial and Federal Acts of Parliament, and have examined the results produced by Temperance organizations throughout the Dominion. The conclusions reached appear in separate pamphlets. They deal with the situation in British Columbia, the Prairie Provinces, Ontario, Quebec and the Maritime Provinces.

These documents show the powerful hold the liquor traffic has had on Canadian Life. They unfold a long, sad story of crime, sorrow and misery. The gradual rise of indignation on the part of the Canadian people against the ravages of alcohol is traced and accurate statements of the present situation are presented.

Phenomenal progress has been made by the advocates of prohibition in Canada during the past decade. It was a distinct advance to secure the abolition of the "open" bar. Commercial considerations alone make it impossible for the "bar" as an institution to reappear. Another encouraging feature has been the quiet but effective way in which objections to prohibitory laws have been overcome. It was said that proper hotel accommodation could not be maintained. This objection is not urged to-day. The assertion was made that Prohibition would deprive people of employment. This cry is no longer raised. Prohibition would increase the use of drugs, it was declared. The Honorable Dr. Beland disposed of this contention in his speech in Parliament on the 19th of May last. He reported prosecutions throughout the Provinces last year, for illicit dealing in drugs, to be as follows:—

British Columbia	315
Alberta	91
Saskatchewan	88
Manitoba	15
Ontario	66
New Brunswick	14
Nova Scotia	8
Prince Edward Island	0
Quebec	237

It will be seen that out of 834 convictions, 552 were in the Provinces of British Columbia and Quebec. Again, it was maintained that Prohibition could not be enforced. Existing Prohibition laws in Canada are new, and for that reason, if for no other, will, for a long time, be misunderstood and misrepresented. The enforcement of any law depends on the power of public opinion behind it. Public opinion is formed from statements people believe to be true. Hence the wisdom of presenting facts and contradicting false or exaggerated reports respecting the operation of Prohibition laws.

Three things are a present and pressing necessity in order to hold what has been gained and to move to still higher ground:—

First—Propaganda. Full publicity must be given to the benefits already secured by the present prohibitory laws.

Second—Education. Apart from the moral issues involved, what a wealth of material is available for this purpose!

For example—

1. Scientific facts proved by observation and experiment.

2. Statistics gathered by trustworthy agencies.

3. Economic data as to the efficiency of workers who do not use alcohol.

4. Startling differences between "dry" and "wet" communities.

The younger generation must be shown in public school and Sunday School, the deadly effects of alcohol. They must know the history of struggles endured by their parents to liberate Canada from a ruthless tyranny which has always accompanied the traffic in strong drink.

Third—Co-operation. It must be regarded as a national obligation resting on all good citizens to assist in the enforcement of prohibition laws which were enacted following a direct mandate of the people.

These pamphlets are sent out, therefore, in the hope that they may help to deliver Canada from an evil which, because of its nature, is an enemy of human happiness and a barrier to national progress.

D. N. McLACHLAN,

For the Board of Home Missions
and Social Service.

THE LIQUOR TRAFFIC IN THE PROVINCE OF QUEBEC.

By R. L. Werry, Secretary, The Anti-Liquor League of the Province of Quebec.

Tragedy marks every page of the history of the struggle of the temperance forces against the demon of strong drink in the Province of Quebec. Wrecked homes are the heart-breaking evidences of domestic tragedy. Lost and wasted millions measure the economic tragedy everywhere manifested in the poverty, ignorance, squalor and vice of the slums. Moral tragedy is evidenced by the absolute lack of appreciation or realization, in wide circles, of the evil inherent in the use of and commerce in alcoholic beverages, entirely apart from its effects on the human body or on human environment.

Great as is the tragedy resulting from the use and the abuse of alcoholic liquor, still more tragic is the fact that our legislators seem to be unable or unwilling to see the social tragedy in its grim reality or to devise and enact measures that would effectively deal with and ameliorate the situation. This is the sad and amazing fact as will be revealed below:

In no province of Canada is the History of the Temperance Movement more interesting or more complicated—or the present situation more serious—than in the Province of Quebec. A review of the progress of this cause, to be complete, must go back over a period of three centuries and would include education, legislation and agitation in great variety. English and French, Catholic and Protestant agencies and influences have combined, sometimes separately and occasionally quite unitedly, to bring public sentiment and statutory enactments on temperance questions to the position we find them in to-day.

Territory 90 Per Cent. Dry.

The investigator and the historian will find many apparent paradoxes in the process of ferreting out the facts that go to complete the story of the evolution of temperance legislation in Quebec Province. He will find that, while public sentiment is to-day declared to be against prohibition throughout the province, it was in this province that the first prohibitory regulations known in the territory comprising the Dominion were enacted and enforced. More surprising still is the fact that in spite of loud protestations against the tyranny of prohibition and persistent demands for greater liberty for the advocates of intoxicating beverages, 1,097 municipalities out of 1,187 in this province in 1917 had no licenses and in them little, if any, liquor was sold or used—certainly none legally. That is to say, territorially over 92 per cent. of Quebec Province is "dry" while the large towns and cities, thanks to the facilities granted them, or rather **forced upon them,** by the present government, are the wettest spots on the North American Continent. The events leading up to these conditions will be both interesting and edifying to recount, even briefly, as they must be in a small brochure.

Pere de Rochemonteix is the authority for a statement, in a History of "The Jesuits and New France in

2

the 17th Century," that drunkenness among the Indians was not heard of until after the taking of Quebec by the English in 1629. It is admitted that French fur-traders coming to Canada in 1632 found the sale and consumption of liquor already established and took advantage of this trade to add to their profits, brandy being dealt in to a large extent in spite of the express prohibition by the Governors and opposition by the Church. The Jesuit Fathers were particularly pronounced in their denunciation of the traffic and their missionaries held the first temperance meeting on this continent, so far as records show, at Sillery, near Quebec City, in the summer of 1648.

First Prohibitory Law.

It is further recorded that on March 7th, 1657, an edict was issued by Louis XIV. prohibiting all sale of liquor to the Indians especially and in general "to all ranks and classes in the community whether high or low." The penalty for violations of this decree included corporal punishment and a heavy fine which was to be divided equally—one-third to the informer, one-third to the Hotel Dieu (hospital) and one-third to the Royal Treasury. The culprit in addition came under the censure of the Church. Bishop Laval in 1660 proclaimed that all Catholics who indulged or engaged in the traffic should be excommunicated; if he thought them deserving they might be put to death; and he alone could grant them absolution in special cases.

This had a very salutary effect for a short time. The Governor, in order to please those interested in the liquor traffic, failed to enforce the law and a serious reaction developed scenes of vice and violence accompanied by gross immorality, lawlessness and opposition to the Church. Finally the Fathers of the Sorbonne in France were appealed to by the King for their decision. They pronounced the traffic in strong liquor to be a mortal sin. Many prohibitory enactments were made and soon after rescinded as better influences either gained the ascendency or were repressed. One priest in 1666 wrote: "All our Indian villages are so many taverns for drunkenness and Sodoms of Iniquity."

A French traveller after visiting Canada about 1690 declared, "All the rascals and idlers in the country are attracted into the business of tavern-keeping. They never dream of tilling the soil but on the contrary they deter other inhabitants from it and end with ruining them."

Has the traffic improved one whit in the three centuries of Canadian History? Is alcohol less deadly?

License System Started.

The licensing system as at present administered may be said to date from 1774 when the Quebec Revenue Act was passed by the Imperial Government "to establish a fund towards defraying the charges of the administration." Provision was thus made for the granting by the Governor, Lieutenant-Governor or Commander-in-Chief of the Province of a license for the keeping of houses of entertainment and for the retailing of wine, brandy, rum or any other spirituous liquors. The license was one pound, sixteen shillings.

4

The penalty for selling without license was ten pounds. In 1795 the license fee was raised to two pounds, payable annually. In 1805 the sale of wine and spirits on Sunday was prohibited—except for sick persons or to travellers with meals.

In 1850 tavern keepers were subjected to a fine and imprisonment in case accidents happened to intoxicated persons to whom they sold liquor! The legislature also placed the licensing authority in the hands of the Church Warden, the Senior Magistrate, and the Senior Military Authority.

Although the authorities continued to provide for the sale of intoxicating liquors they always recognized the evils of intemperance and saw the desirability of minimizing the abuses which always accompanied indulgence in alcoholic beverages.

Evidence of this is seen in the passing, about the year 1851 of "An Act for the more effective suppression of Intemperance." The provisions of this Act required that an applicant for a license must secure a requisition signed by a majority of the municipal electors declaring that a tavern was necessary at the place applied for. The applicant was further required to own a certain amount of real or personal property, provide security for $500.00 and two sureties for $250.00 each. The applicant had also to procure a certificate of "unblemished reputation" signed by two Justices of the Peace, or ten municipal electors. Fifty dollars was the amount of the license fee at this time. Under this act a penalty was fixed for persons arrested for drunkenness, and it became necessary for a person to secure the signatures of twenty-five electors to his application before he could secure a license. In 1853 this clause was amended for the cities of Montreal and Quebec requiring fifty names of the electors on the application for a license. The effects of these regulations were to establish the liquor business on a more or less respectable basis, to create a sort of vested right in a license and to produce a considerable revenue for the Government, all of which tended to perpetuate the evil without appreciably reducing drinking or its consequences—Poverty and Crime.

An Apostle of Temperance.

Brief reference must be made here to the magnificent work of Reverend Father Chiniquy, who in 1838, when Abbe of Beauport, near the City of Quebec, began a crusade in the interest of temperance; three years of hard work brought him the blessing of the Bishop of Nancy who, on arriving in Canada for a visit, advised the consecration of the priest to a great temperance mission. Within four years he had won more than twenty parishes over to temperance both in principle and practice, by his teachings regarding the effects of alcohol on body and soul. In 1848-49 he visited 120 parishes and won more than two hundred thousand converts to total abstinence according to records kept at the time. The effects of this campaign remain to this day.

Other agencies sprang up to perpetuate and extend the good work. In 1847 the Sons of Temperance order was planted in Quebec and Eastern Canada, being introduced by members from the United States where it was founded in New York City, September 29th, 1842. The Independent (now International) Order of Good Templars followed about 1857, and the Royal Templars of Temperance began operations in 1878 in Ontario and about 1885 in Quebec Province.

The W.C.T.U. dates its origin from early in 1874 when the first Union was formed at Chautauqua, N.Y. The first Union in Canada is said to have been instituted at Owen Sound, Ontario, in May of the same year, and the first Union in Quebec Province was formed at Stanstead in 1877.

Revival of Activities.

The Quebec Branch of the Dominion Alliance was organized in 1879 with the avowed object of bringing about the suppression of the liquor traffic. Its work has been along educational, legislative and law-enforcement lines and probably its greatest success was achieved in securing local option throughout the English sections of the province and opposing the granting of licenses in polling subdivisions in the cities, which was provided for by the Quebec Temperance Act and the Canada Temperance Act, commonly known as the Scott Act.

In 1914 the Anti-Liquor League of the Province of Quebec was organized with similar objects, and in March, 1919, a Union Temperance Convention was called when a Federation of the temperance forces was effected, the Executive of which became the Quebec Campaign Committee, whose first act was to fight the beer and wine amendments to the Prohibition Law passed in March, to come into effect May, 1st, 1919.

Voting on the Referendum took place on April 10th, about three weeks after the Convention and the amendment in favour of beer and wine was carried.

The "Ligue Anti-Alcoolique," a French organization, had been co-operating quite heartily with the English temperance forces for several years, but in this instance some of their members who favoured wine and beer refused to join in the campaign and no temperance work has been done by them since. In fact the temperance people generally throughout the Province seem to be standing aside to see what the Government will do and whether their professions of giving the Province temperance legislation will be made good in fact.

It is well understood that without the co-operation and actual leadership of the Roman Catholic Church Authorities and Catholic temperance organizations no effective legislation can be secured in Quebec Province. Up to the year 1906 the work of temperance organizations had been chiefly educational and their gatherings had been largely of a social character.

In 1905, after several conferences between representatives of the Dominion Alliance and Archbishop Bruchesi, his Grace launched a remarkably successful pledge-signing campaign. The Franciscan Fathers were commissioned to conduct the temperance mission, and as a result of a few months' efforts, beginning in February, 1906, it is reported that 39,765 men, 32,070 women and 9,280 children signed the total-abstinence pledge. It was said that of the men, 20,863 were heads of families. This work covered about 100 parishes. Archbishop Begin, of Quebec, and a number of Bishops

8

in various parts of the Province supported the movement most heartily. It was in 1906 that the Ligue Anti-Alcoolique of Quebec (City) was formed, and in 1907 the Montreal Branch was organized.

Temperance Amendments.

Several important amendments to the Quebec License Law followed at the Session of the Legislature in 1907:

The employment of bar-maids in hotels and restaurants was prohibited.

Distillers' licenses were increased from $250.00 to $1,000.00; brewers' from $200.00 to $750.00.

Retail license fees were revised and increased.

It was made illegal to sell or supply intoxicants in clubs to persons under 21 years of age, or in restaurants under 18 years.

In 1908 the Legislature at the request of the combined French and English organizations made further amendments among which were the following:

License holders were forbidden to cash or exchange workmen's cheques.

The number of licenses was reduced in Montreal, Quebec and other cities.

The sale of liquor on Christmas, New Years and Good Friday was prohibited.

On May 1st, 1911, the famous early-closing law came into force when liquor-selling establishments were obliged to shut their doors at 7 p.m. on Saturday nights and 11 p.m. on all other week-nights and not open again until 7 a.m. on the next week-day. In country districts the week-night closing hour was 10 o'clock.

The Liquor License Law of 1914 consolidated the ·Provincial temperance legislation and marked further advances. A review of this Act (section 14 of the 5th Chapter of Title 4 of the Revised Statutes of 1909 with amendments), reveals the following restrictions:

The bringing of intoxicating liquors into any mine or mining premises was forbidden.

Drinking any intoxicating liquor in any mine or in any dependencies thereof was prohibited.

Licenses were not to be given for any premises within two hundred feet of a church, school, convent, etc.

Section 1029 provided that "No grocer or dealer in articles of food shall sell or keep for sale in the building, wherein his groceries or food products are kept, any intoxicating liquor. . . ." after May 1st, 1915.

Licenses for the sale of liquor by grocers could be issued only to persons already holding liquor-grocery licenses and the liquor business must be kept entirely separate from the grocery business. This restriction led a number of grocers to give up keeping liquor altogether.

No person under eighteen years of age could be employed to act as bar tender in any licensed establishment, and no female, except the wife of the keeper of

10

a hotel or restaurant, could act as bar-maid or wait on the guests in any public place where liquor was sold.

It was forbidden to sell liquor on Labour Day and Dominion Day as well as New Years, Christmas and Good Friday.

The hour for opening bars and restaurants for the sale of liquor was fixed at 7.30 a.m., and the municipal councils of cities and towns were given power to pass by-laws closing all bars at 10 instead of 11 p.m., and keeping them closed until 7 a.m. On Saturdays they had still to close at 7 p.m.

An applicant for a license had to obtain the signatures of twenty-five municipal electors resident in his polling subdivision before he could obtain a certificate and a majority opposition was sufficient to prevent a license being granted.

License commssioners approved the license certificates in the cities of Montreal and Quebec while the Mayor and City Clerk or Secretary-Treasurer of the Council had to approve of the same in all other municipalities.

License Reduction.

One of the most important sections of this Act provided for the gradual reduction in the number of licenses in certain places as under: Beginning May 1st, 1915, "the number of certificates for licenses of inns and restaurants which may be confirmed or granted within the City of Quebec shall be limited to a maximum of fifty; for Montreal the maximum shall be four hundred; and (reduced) to a minimum of 350 for year beginning May 1st, 1916." Licenses lapsing for any cause were not to be replaced. The number of licenses in adjoining municipalities in the case of their being annexed could not exceed the number existing at the time of annexation.

The license fees were to be increased in the same proportion as the numbers were decreased in order that the revenue might remain the same as before. It was arranged that persons who lost their licenses owing to this reduction should receive compensation.

The maximum number of licenses that might be granted in other towns and cities throughout the Province was fixed. The number of retail liquor stores was also fixed.

After paying indemnities for a couple of years the Government found the compensation system defective and impossible to maintain and no further indemnities were granted while this law remained in force.

This law was considered by the temperance people to be the most satisfactory ever enacted in this Province. Drinking opportunities were reduced almost to a minimum, and it was fondly believed that with a little more faithful educational work and the further extension of local option, the threshold of prohibition would be reached.

The year 1916 saw another agressive campaign for Provincial Prohibition. On October 4th a strong deputation waited on the Premier, Sir Lomer Gouin, and his cabinet, and urged speedy action in this regard. As a result more stringent enactments were passed at the 1916-17 session. The number of licensed places was further reduced, and treating was prohibited (but unfortunately not abolished). Bars could be opened only at 9 a.m. and were obliged to close at 7 p.m. on Saturdays and 9 o'clock every other night in the week. It was further decided that bar-rooms should give place to cafes in May, 1918.

Quebec City Voted Dry.

On October 4th, 1917, the City of Quebec voted for Prohibition under the provisions of the Canada Temperance Act. The Protestant workers of that city had just previously been organized as the Quebec Temperance Union. These joined heartily with the leading citizens and clergy of the Roman Catholic Church with the result that at the close of the poll it was found that there was a majority for Prohibition of 3,251. The law became effective on May 1st, 1918, closing 40 bars and 70 licensed groceries.

A caucus of Quebec Provincial Liberals was held in January, 1918, to consider the situation created by the Dominion Order-in-Council re War Time Prohibition and the advisability of enacting a Provincial Prohibition law. Premier Gouin suggested total Prohibition to take effect within a year's time, thus giving dealers sufficient delay in which to dispose of their stocks.

J. N. Francoeur, member for Lotbiniere, expressed himself as in favour of prohibiting hard liquors but suggested that wine and beer should be allowed. Peter Bercovitch, K.C., member for St. Louis Division, Montreal, proposed that a referendum be taken on the question. Both suggestions were received in silence and the decision was left with the Government.

The Cabinet in due time agreed to introduce a Prohibition law at the 1919 session, but in the meantime the liquor forces got busy stirring up public opinion, in favour of a referendum, and to have an amendment to the dry law that would permit the sale of wine and beer.

Beer and Wine Referendum.

At a Provincial Prohibition convention held in Montreal March 13th, 1919, a strong resolution in favour of bone-dry Prohibition and against any amendments to allow wine and beer was passed and forwarded to Quebec where the house was in session. However, a few days later the Government announced that a referendum would be held on April 10th, only three weeks away. A campaign was organized for educational purposes rather than with much expectation of success. The Roman Catholic Church took no part and had no voice in this campaign. If the temperance forces had anticipated having to fight without the support of the Church it is probable they would have allowed the referendum to go by default which many advocated at the time.

The question voted on was, "Is it your opinion that the sale of light beer, cider and wines, as defined by law, should be allowed?" The result was 178,112 votes recorded for and 48,413 against beer and wine.

On March 17th, 1919, assent was given to the Quebec Prohibition Law. It was provided therein that "authorized vendors" should have the privilege of selling wines for sacramental purposes and alcoholic liquors solely for medicinal, mechanical, industrial, scientific and artistic purposes. None of these liquors could be drunk on the premises where they were sold. None of the wares could be advertised or displayed for sale and all packages containing liquor must bear a label indicating the nature of the contents together with the name and address of the maker.

Beer and wine licenses were provided for in the guise of "temperance drinks." The proviso under which the referendum was taken stipulated that "light beer, cider and wine mean beer and other malt liquors containing not more than 2.51 per cent. of alcohol, weight measure, and cider and wine containing not more than 6.94 per cent. of alcohol, weight measure. Anything stronger than this could only be sold by the "Vendors," and that under strict regulations as to certificates from authorized purchasers stating the purpose for which the purchase was made. For instance, one clause said, "if the sale is of intoxicating liquors for medicinal purposes, such certificate shall be given by the attending physician setting forth the date, names and addresses of patient and physician, naming quantity and kind of liquor and declaring that it was for medicinal purposes only. Similar regulations surrounded the sales of industrial and mechanical liquors, all of which, needless to say, were frequently circumvented.

Alcoholic Liquor Act.

It is well-known that the "Vendors" heaped up fortunes said to amount to millions of dollars in some instances during the time in which they carried on their business. "Temperance licenses" were often merely blinds for the surreptitious sale of hard stuff, and evasions of the law were so numerous, so flagrant and so easy to accomplish that the Government in despair decided to change conditions by bringing in an entirely new law on the principle of Government ownership and control under the name of the Alcoholic Liquor Act. This Act was assented to on February 25th, 1921, and came into effect on May 1st following.

By this law all hard liquor, including wine, is sold by a Liquor Commission, while beer is sold to dealers by the brewers who pay to the Government a tax of 5 per cent. on all their sales. Hard liquor is sold (retail) by agents of the Commission from commissioners' stores; or from their warehouses in wholesale quantities; beer may be sold in restaurants, (cafes), where it is served at tables instead of bars. Wine and beer may be served, with meals only, in eating-houses and hotels. Under the various regulations, however, it is found that every kind of liquor may be had in any desired quantity on any possible occasion required, legitimately if one goes the right way about it; and there are many loopholes that are taken advantage of by bootleggers and others who make their living by illegal traffic. In fact the present law lends itself to a great many abuses that were almost unknown under the old license laws.

Beer saloons, as understood in old license days, are now called taverns. It is not required to sell food with beer in these places. What used to be called the barroom of a hotel is now designated a tavern. Liquor may be sold with meals in the dining-rooms of boats and clubs and trains and other establishments or places recognized as dining-rooms by the Commission. Liquor stores can be established for the sale of beer and wine only. A license for a banquet costs ten dollars. A six-months' permit can be obtained for hotels at summer resorts, for restaurants and beer gardens and dance halls. The Commissioners' stores are open from 9 a.m. until 6 p.m. every day except that they close at 1 p.m. on Saturdays and do not open again until Monday morning.

Brewers cannot sell or deliver before 7 a.m. nor after 6 p.m. Stores and taverns are forbidden to sell or deliver beer before 9 a.m. or after 10 p.m., and the

same hours apply to places that serve wine or beer during meals. It is forbidden to sell any liquor on Sundays, New Year's Day, Epiphany, Ash Wednesday, Good Friday, Ascension Day, All Saints' Day, Conception Day or Christmas Day; or in the territory in which an election is being held, on the day of voting for members of municipal councils, Dominion Parliament or Provincial Legislature.

Commission Autocratic.

The Quebec Liquor Commission are masters of the situation in almost every respect. They have absolute powers as to the granting of any licenses to any persons for any place for any length of time within a year. They have sole discretion as to the fixtures and accommodation that shall be provided in hotels, restaurants, cafes, etc., where liquor is sold. The only important restrictions placed upon them are the following: The Commission must refuse to grant any permit (license) in any municipality where a prohibitory by-law is in force; or in any municipality whose council has by by-law requested the Commission to refuse to grant any permit—provided that such by-law be filed at the office of the Commission at a specified time. The Commission must also refuse to grant a permit for the sale of alcoholic liquor upon the grounds occupied by any agricultural or industrial exhibition or any race meeting. This can be overcome, however, by parties interested forming a club and securing a club license. All permits expire automatically on the 30th of April in each year and any license may be cancelled without notice, if, in the opinion of the Commissioners, their holder commits an offence to merit its withdrawal. There is local option for rural municipalities as above indicated, but there is no means by which the rate-payers can prevent the granting of permits in the cities of Montreal or Quebec, for example. As a matter of fact, permits have been granted in many sections of the city of Montreal, where formerly all bar licenses had been cleaned out by majority opposition petitions in the polling subdivisions. Temperance workers, again and again, have pleaded with the present Government; but in vain, for the restoration of this form of local option or, better still, for a vote to be taken on the question by wards at the regular municipal elections. Apparently the Government is afraid of the consequences of such a vote, since they refuse to take up the challenge of the temperance people on this point.

Grounds For Opposition.

The opposition of the temperance people to the present law and their reasons for the same have been stated clearly and briefly in the following resolution:

"We hereby place ourselves on record as being totally opposed to the Quebec Liquor Law as at present administered, (a) because of the arbitrary powers vested in the Liquor Commission, (b) because the right of citizens to oppose the establishment of licensed places in certain large towns and cities has been abolished, (c) because there is no limit to the number of licenses or permits that may be granted, (d) because the strength of alcoholic beverages has been increased without the approval of the electors or the citizens in general, (e) because it is made the channel for raising revenue for the public services of the Province, (f) because the sale and consumption of all kinds of intoxicating drinks, according to Government reports, have rather increased than decreased under this system."

All the restrictions and safeguards that had been secured by years of agitation were shattered; all the efforts for reducing the strength of alcoholic beverages counted for nothing; all the toil expended in securing the reduction in the number of licensed places and driving the traffic out of residential districts was negatived, when the Commission was given autocratic and exclusive powers in these respects.

Offence Against Democracy.

But the greatest offence against democracy and the greatest usurpation of powers that should belong to a free and intelligent electorate were committed when the Government tore up that scrap of paper known as the Quebec Prohibition Law and without consent or vote of the people authorized the sale of hard liquor, first through authorized vendors and later through the agency of the Liquor Commission. It is indisputable that the wine and beer referendum was an absolute fiasco, being in no sense "vox populi." But there was not even a semblance or pretence of right behind the act of restoring the sale of hard liquor as at present carried on.

It was pretended on behalf of the Government that the present law was a distinctly temperance measure. Whether it is such or not, can be best judged by the results of the trade carried on by the Commission and recorded by them. One of their first reports said:

"From May 1st to December 31st (1921), the sales totalled $9,325,727.41 as follows:—

"May, $280,173.39; June, $466,243.92; July, $729,-

19

007.44; August, $1,029,996.30; September, $1,115,-
695.75; October, $1,225,908.50; November, $1,564,-
760.80; December, $2,470,295.35, and by mail from
Montreal $406,021, from Quebec $43,224.96."

Some record, indeed! By way of explanation and
perhaps to disarm criticism from certain quarters, the
report added:

"Much of the liquor has been sold to outsiders,
hundreds of thousands of visitors coming into the
Province to enjoy a little liberty (?) not to cause dis-
order (?) and it has been estimated that 84 per cent.
of the liquor sold in Montreal had been sold to people
outside the province!!"

As a further palliation to tender consciences it
was vouchsafed that the profits would go principally to
good roads, education, charity, etc.

Drink Bill Over $30,000,000.

In a report to the Quebec Legislature in session
on October 31st, it was made known that for the year
ending April 30th last, the net revenue to the Commission was $4,000,974.50, of which the Government had
received $3,892,398.95, leaving a surplus of $108,575.55
in the hands of the Commission. This net revenue in-
cludes profits of $2,860,010.64 and income from profits,
fines, seizures, etc., $1,140,963.86. The sales amounted
to $15,212,801.21.

The purchases of liquor amounted to $15,632,-
335.00, less the amount of inventory on April 30th last,
which was $5,540,790.07.

The sales of beer by brewers to taverns totalled
$15,684,670.63—the total quantity sold was 22,563,-
008 gallons—and the 5 per cent. tax brought in $784,-
233.53.

Of this, beer manufactured and sold in the **Province** amounted to 21,741,964 gallons costing $15,050,-819.19, and imported from Ontario 579,385 gallons valued at $467,134.78. Beer exported from Quebec amounted to 241,660 gallons valued at $166,716.66. The Royal road to total abstinence!

It is interesting to note the extreme abstemiousness of the people of Quebec City on New Year's Eve, 1921, as reported in a despatch from that city which said:

"It is estimated that over $75,000.00 worth of liquor was sold in the six Quebec Liquor Commission stores from 9 a.m. until 1 p.m. on New Year's Eve, this being the record business ever recorded by the Liquor Depots here. Though requests had been made to the Liquor Commissioners asking for extra hours last Saturday to meet the enormous demand, this was not granted, and from 12 to to 1 the stores were so crowded that many had to wait hopefully in the cold for their turn to go in."

On January 3rd, 1922, a Montreal paper announced that 1,065 permits for the sale of beer in taverns and grocery stores had been granted by the Commission as against about 800 in the previous year. It was recently stated in the House that 296 tavern permits were granted in Montreal in 1921, and 307 on or since May 1st, 1922. The balance of permits were for grocery and other miscellaneous privileges. The smallest number of licenses for bars under the old license law was 200 as fixed by statute for the year beginning May 1st, 1918. Licensed groceries reached the minimum of 200 also on May 1st, 1918. In 1921 it was officially stated that in only 232 out of the 1,315 municipalities comprised in the Province were beer and wine permits granted, and that the Commission at that time was operating 64 stores for the sale of wine and hard liquors. While this looks somewhat favourable yet the fact remains that facilities for obtaining intoxicating liquors are far too numerous. The alarming fact is that the taverns everywhere are full nightly with old and young men sitting at tables sipping beer and chattering maudlin gibberish that is neither edifying nor instructive. Employers report that these men are often unfit for their duties the next day and many men fail to report for work on one or more mornings of the week as a result of over-indulgence.

Pour on Oil to Stop Fire.

The Government has announced that its settled policy, born of a conviction that it is a wise decision, is to encourage the drinking of wine and beer in order to bring about a decrease in the consumption of hard liquor. If ever a principle was proved to be fallacious both by science and by experience, this one has been most emphatically. The alcoholic element in all these beverages creates an appetite which only grows by what it feeds upon and can never be cured or satisfied by its continued use in whatever quantity taken.

Temperance people and the public in general had a right to expect that when the Government took over the liquor business with the avowed intention of promoting temperance that some members of the Commission would be recognized temperance advocates and that educational propaganda would be carried on with the object of emphasizing the evils of the traffic which was admittedly difficult to curb or control. Any who had such expectations were doomed to disappointment for there is not a single member of the Commission who is in favour of the suppression of the traffic and not a word has escaped from lip or pen of one of them in favour of total abstinence or even moderation. On the other hand quite recently advertisements have appeared in the newspapers quoting supposedly eminent physicians favouring the use of wine.

Another phase of the Government's policy which is regarded by all temperance people as unsound, both morally and economically, is the openly admitted object it has of making money out of the traffic for public services such as good roads, education, charity, etc. It is pitiable in this age of the world to see a Government making money out of human frailty, ruined homes and immortal souls even for legitimate objects. The motto seems to have been adopted of doing evil that good may come. The old saying still holds true: "What is morally wrong can never be made legally right."

Owner, But Cannot Control.

Much has been said on the subject of Government ownership and control of the liquor traffic. There are those who denounce the system as identifying the people more closely with the vile business than even the old license system. Others as strongly repudiate and deny this view of the matter. The fact is that no one who is openly and consistently opposed to the liquor business can be held responsible for its continuance under whatever system. If the Government were using its power as owning and controlling the traffic gradually to suppress it and, as speedily as possible, abolish it, all the while raising public sentiment up to the ideal of voluntary personal abstinence there would be only praise for it—which proves that the fault is not inherent in the ownership but in the use made of the powers enjoyed.

Government ownership and control place in the hands of the people's representatives the power to strangle the greatest foe that torments and demoralizes the citizens of Canada to-day. Properly administered its principles would make the liquor traffic within twelve months but the memory of a nightmare and open the road to reconstructed homes and happy family life. Badly administered, Government control of the liquor traffic opens the road to political patronage, graft, villanies, immoralities and abuses more disgraceful and monstrous than have yet blotted the pages of this country's history. This is the issue and the grave responsibility that rests upon the shoulders of the Quebec Government.

The present law is not wholly bad, many restrictions imposed are wholesome and fully appreciated by the temperance people, but they are far outweighed by the defects and the loss of power the anti-liquor forces formerly possessed of gradually driving the enemy off the map.

Making Smooth Road to Perdition.

In order that no person may be deprived of his favourite beverages we have, in addition to the sale of wine and hard liquor by the Commission direct, permits for taverns, restaurants, groceries, clubs, beer gardens, dance halls, summer hotels, boats, trains, etc. Quite recently several wine stores were opened in

24

Montreal exclusively for the accommodation of "Ladies" who wish to buy their favourite beverages without having to mingle with men in the regular liquor stores.

Sir William Stavert, a member of the Liquor Commission, in an interview in a Montreal paper last August, said: "It would be well to influence the popular favour away from liquors of high strength and towards the use of lighter wines." If the Commission were succeeding in this direction there would not be the immense demand for hard liquors that their reports show. Besides the law has removed the limit of strength for both beer and wine that may be sold for all purposes, and every effort is being made to meet the demands of customers, regardless of potency.

In the same interview it was intimated that "to serve the demands of other classes of clients vodka and Chinese liquors have been placed on sale in various shops."

A few weeks earlier it was announced by the Chairman of the Commission, Honourable George A. Simard, that "the various sales depend to a very large extent on the district in which the liquors are sold. For instance, in the lower part of the city the great bulk of the sales consists of hard liquor. The manager of one of the stores stated that over twenty per cent. of the gin sold in his district is purchased by Chinese. In the uptown districts, it is claimed, wines are much more in demand."

For the expression of a "temperance man" at the head of such a "temperance organization" as the Government selling agency, the following is really rich: "Little by little our wines are becoming known or rather appreciated by the public, and during the last few months of the year the wine sales have been comparatively much higher. Certain brands of claret and sauternes and especially domestic brands sold in bulk or by the gallon have become very big sellers; and the South European habit of drinking wine with meals is likely to become popular in this part of the country."

Now let us turn to the other side of the picture. What are the actual results of the liquor law and what are the opinions of those who are watching its operation in the interest of the public—from the outside?

Pertinent Comment.

Recorder Semple, whose court deals with the usual offences growing out of indulgence in liquor, on October 17th, 1922, declared in connection with a case before him:

"These husband-and-wife cases have got to stop. We are far too lenient with these cases. We do not send the men to Bordeaux, because if we did their wives and children would starve. If we could only get 50 cents a day for prison labour, Bordeaux jail would not be big enough to hold all the men I could send there in twelve months. Yesterday afternoon I had seven applications from women for warrants against their husbands. The husbands put the blame on the women. Who takes the money on Friday and goes into the saloon and stays there until all his money is gone? Who drinks? The woman? No, the man. And what does the man say? 'I am going to have my beer; nobody can stop me from having my beer.'"

The use of narcotic drugs has been exposed with unusual emphasis in Montreal of late. (Strange that it is not recognized by the authorities that alcohol is one of the most insidious and destructive of narcotics!)

The tavern keepers now have been organized into the newest battery of the crusade against narcotic-drug peddling. Special orders have been issued by the Licensed Victuallers' Association to all proprietors of taverns to maintain a strict watch over those who are permitted to sit at tavern tables. All persons who have convictions registered against them for drug peddling are to be ordered out and those suspected of being peddlers are to be closely watched and reported to the police immediately their conduct justifies action.

An Alarming Report.

The Montreal Standard recently sent its reporters out for a story on life in the dives of the city connected with the beer saloon. Following are brief extracts from a most alarming report:

"Pocket-edition raids on night cafes is one of the latest activities taken up by plain-clothes police who are determined that the city shall be purged of the shady restaurant proprietor who lets groups of lads and girls gather for hours in private rooms where they indulge in risque conversation and "advanced" story-telling.

"Five times in the last ten days one restaurant has been raided in this way. Each time the raiding squad has found from eight to a dozen youths and girls of ages ranging from 14 to 19 piled into a private room designed for four people, and in this restaurant there are several of such rooms.

"A black list of twenty-seven cafes of this character went to Quebec last year. For four months these cafes were closed. Then they got provincial licenses owing to the fact that the city police had reported the cafes by street number only. The restaurant proprietors changed and new permits were given."

The same paper reports that gambling to a great extent is indulged in or promoted in these taverns and remarks that games of chance have greatly increased since bars were done away with owing to the facilities which the tables afford.

It is the opinion of temperance people that the present liquor law could not suit the liquor dealers better if it had been drawn by their solicitor. But it appears that the dealers are not yet satisfied. A deputation recently waited on the Government at Quebec and asked for amendments that would enable hotels to serve beer and wine to guests in their rooms. Tavern and restaurant proprietors want a dual license to authorize the sale of both wine and beer; and grocers are said to want the privilege of selling wine as well as beer. These requests will be opposed by the temperance people.

Views of Temperance Folk.

To show how general and widespread is the dissatisfaction with the present law among temperance people the following opinions may be quoted:

The Montreal Witness says: "The Quebec Liquor Law has a number of excellent provisions but as a whole it appals us."

Rev. W. D. Reid, D.D., Minister of Stanley Presbyterian Church, in a sermon on the question, 'Is the Quebec Government a successful bartender?' said:

"It certainly is if the business is viewed from a question of dollars and cents and from the angle of making drunkards." Dr. Reid claimed that it was one of the greatest calamities imaginable when a Government instead of trying to lift up a people went into the business of degrading them. It simply meant a Government making money out of the weaknesses of the people. "Montreal is becoming the dumping ground for all the riff-raff of the Continent of America," said Rev. Dr. Reid.

Rev. J. R. Dobson, Minister of St. Giles' Presbyterian Church, preaching on national evils, quoted from the prophet Isaiah who 2,600 years ago denounced the traffic in strong drink along four lines—1st, it led the nation into captivity; 2nd, it caused hell to open its mouth so wide that multitudes of all classes of society were engulfed; 3rd, it was the fertile mother of many other national and social evils; 4th, it blunted the moral sense of the people both high and low. This was the traffic which the Quebec Government was interested in promoting.

R. L. Werry, Secretary of the Anti-Liquor League of the Province of Quebec, says: "We have the spectacle of a Government spending thousands of dollars on a health department to combat fevers, tuberculosis, cancer and smallpox, confiscating decayed and adulterated food and taking other commendable measures to promote public health, while at the same time it is deliberately giving permits for the sake of revenue to hundreds of persons to dispense a most deadly poison to their fellow citizens as a means of making a living. Every beer, wine and whisky tap is a poisoned well. Habitual drunkenness is a recognized vice and any Government that makes money out of a business that makes drunkards is profiting by commercialized vice. Drunkard-making is more immoral and more inhuman than the slave trade."

S. J. Carter, President of the Quebec Branch of the Dominion Alliance, declares: "There is in my mind no doubt that in the Quebec Liquor Act we have lost ground and are rapidly drifting back to where we were many years ago. We have only words of condemnation for the action of our Provincial Government which, existing theoretically to promote the happiness and welfare of all the citizens, has chosen to enrich its treasury by means of a business that dissipates happiness, debauches the individual and has ever been the close ally of the other enemies of society."

In the Quebec Legislature, in the last week of the month of December, 1922, near the close of the session, Premier Taschereau declared that "the (Liquor) law had been a success both from a moral and material point of view; he expressed pride in the superb work of the (Liquor) Commission and said that the law was to be continued. . . . On the moral side the Premier remarked: Where were those delegations of the clergy and prohibition societies and others who had been wont to come to Quebec? They had not been seen for two years. This he considered good evidence that they were much better satisfied with the new law than they had ever been with the old conditions." (Newspaper report).

The officials of the Anti-Liquor League promptly sent the following telegram to the Premier:

"Church and temperance people strenuously oppose present liquor law on grounds repeatedly laid before you. Useless to send deputations when demands already made are ignored. Government policy regarded as worst possible for Quebec and Canada; and aggravated by new amendments."

As a matter of fact a deputation authorized by a meeting of workers called by the League and representing all the churches, and temperance people generally, waited on the Premier and the Provincial Treasurer in the Government offices in Montreal a year ago and presented a set of regulations including objections to the present law and asking, particularly, for an amendment which would give local option in the cities of the province by wards or polling subdivisions. With this granted they would have been temporarily satisfied. Without it nothing else mattered. The session passed and the request was not granted. Another session has passed and this "standing demand" was not even considered, so far as is known.

It is not surprising, therefore, that there is no disposition on the part of the temperance people to waste their time and money, on jaunts to Quebec. The disposition seems, rather, to be to wait until they can make an appointment with Mr. Taschereau's successor.

The fact that the Taschereau Liquor Law is regarded by temperance people as most un-moral, unpatriotic, un-Christian, un-democratic, impolitic, and devoid of the first elements of true economics shows how diametrically opposed it is to the temperance policy and the temperance people's views of the case. While party politics is not favored by temperance workers it will be the bounden duty of temperance people in this province to help select and elect temperance candidates of either party at the next election. One would be recreant to the highest principles not to do so.

The necessity for a strong, aggressive, educational temperance campaign in Quebec Province was emphasized by Major Horsfall of London, Eng., a delegate to the World Convention Against Alcohol, held recently in Toronto, who has since visited Montreal, when he said:

"The vested interests involved in your big hotels, together with a Government whose principal object in handling the liquor traffic is to make money out of it, make it absolutely necessary to use every means available to suppress the traffic. Every day's delay sees the enemy more firmly entrenched. Under such conditions I do not see how Quebec Province can fail to become the sink-hole of the American continent; and her large cities hotbeds of venereal disease and every species of immorality, crime and degradation known to Sodom. Can you afford to pay this price for a spurious freedom?"

The psychological moment in the history of Quebec Province has arrived when, with the stroke of a pen, her legislators could free every man who is, or soon may be, a victim of the appetite for alcohol. To do this would be to win the plaudits of a nation, the blessing of every woman in the land worthy of her sex, and the approval of every man possessed of a right mind and a proper moral sense. Not to do this will be to call upon their heads the execration of all who shall fall through the inebriating cup and all who shall suffer in consequence of its fateful influence.